the moffatts
backstage pass

By Scott, Clint, Bob & Dave Moffatt
with Elizabeth Weitzman

SCHOLASTIC INC.

New York   Toronto   London   Auckland   Sydney   Mexico City   New Delhi   Hong Kong

Photography Credits:

Front and Back Covers: Anthony Cutajar © 1999; Page 3: Anthony Cutajar © 1999; Page 4: Courtesy of The Moffatts; Page 5: Anthony Cutajar © 1999; Page 6: Courtesy of The Moffatts; Page 7 (top): Janet Macoska; (bottom): Karen Zilch Nadalin © 1999; Page 8: Anthony Cutajar © 1999; Page 9 (top): Karen Zilch Nadalin © 1999; (middle): Courtesy of The Moffatts; (bottom): Janet Macoska; Page 10: Anthony Cutajar © 1999; Page 11 (top): Courtesy of The Moffatts; (bottom): Anthony Cutajar © 1999; Page 12: Anthony Cutajar © 1999; Page 13 (both): Courtesy of The Moffatts; Page 14: Anthony Cutajar © 1999; Page 15 (top): Courtesy of The Moffatts; (bottom): Karen Zilch Nadalin © 1999; Page 16: Karen Zilch Nadalin © 1999; Page 17 (both): Courtesy of The Moffatts; Page 18: Anthony Cutajar © 1999; Page 19 (top left): Karen Zilch Nadalin © 1999; (bottom both): Courtesy of The Moffatts; Page 20: Anthony Cutajar © 1999; Page 21 (top): Karen Zilch Nadalin © 1999; (bottom): Courtesy of The Moffatts; Page 22: Anthony Cutajar © 1999; Page 23 (top): Courtesy of The Moffatts; (bottom): Karen Zilch Nadalin © 1999; Pages 24-25: Anthony Cutajar © 1999; Page 26: Courtesy of The Moffatts; Page 27 (both): Courtesy of The Moffatts; Page 28 (both): Courtesy of The Moffatts; Page 29 (both): Courtesy of The Moffatts; Page 30-31: Courtesy of The Moffatts; Page 32 (top): Anthony Cutajar © 1999; (bottom): Karen Zilch Nadalin © 1999; Page 33: Karen Zilch Nadalin © 1999; Page 34 (top): Karen Zilch Nadalin © 1999; (bottom): Janet Macoska; Page 35: Anthony Cutajar © 1999; Page 36: Karen Zilch Nadalin © 1999; Page 37 (both): Anthony Cutajar © 1999; Page 38: Anthony Cutajar © 1999; Page 39: Karen Zilch Nadalin © 1999; Page 40-41: Anthony Cutajar © 1999; Page 42: Anthony Cutajar © 1999; Page 43 (top): Anthony Cutajar © 1999; (bottom): Karen Zilch Nadalin © 1999; Page 44: Anthony Cutajar © 1999; Page 45 (both): Janet Macoska; Page 46: Anthony Cutajar © 1999; Page 47-48: Courtesy of Capitol Records.

Concert photography by Kai Mueller and Guido Karp for FAN Association. These and other great live photos can be yours as original concert photographs! Simply send an International Reply Coupon (available at every major post office) to the FAN Association Photo Co. c/o The Moffatts, 56200 HoehrOGrenzhausen, Germany, and you shall receive a FANtastic concert photo brochure PLUS a free original live photo of the Moffatts! You may find additional on-line information to this offer at www.fan-association.com

If you purchased this book without a cover, you should be aware that this book is stolen property. It was reported as "unsold and destroyed" to the publisher, and neither the author nor the publisher has received any payment for this "stripped book."

No part of this work may be reproduced, stored in a retrieval system, or transmitted in any form or by any means, electronic, mechanical, photocopying, recording, or otherwise, without written permission of the publisher. For information regarding permission, write to Scholastic Inc., Attention: Permissions Department, 555 Broadway, New York, NY 10012.

ISBN 0-439-13552-4

Design by Peter Koblish

Williams Bell & Associates, Inc.
Personal Management - Nashville, TN

Copyright © 1999 by Scott Andrew Moffatt, Clinton Thomas John Moffatt, Robert Franklin Peter Moffatt, and David Michael Willliam Moffatt. All rights reserved. Published by Scholastic Inc. SCHOLASTIC and associated logos are trademarks and/or registered trademarks of Scholastic Inc.

12 11 10 9 8 7 6 5 4 3 2 1   9/9 0 1 2 3 4/0

Printed in the U.S.A.
First Scholastic printing, September 1999

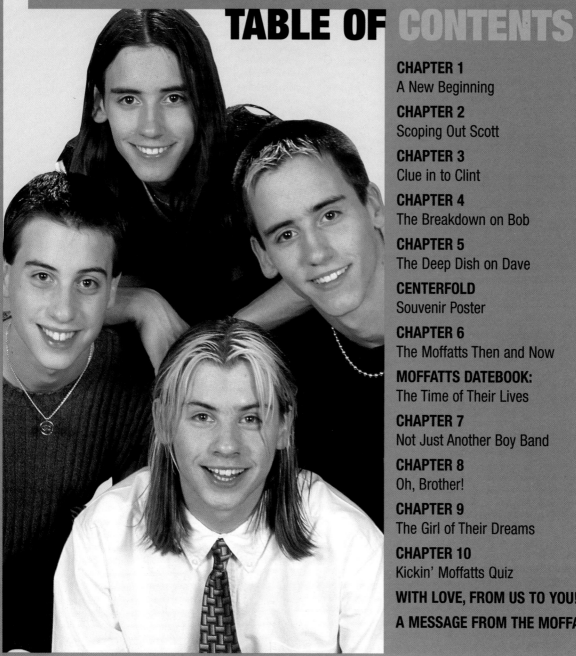

Hi! We're Scott, Clint, Bob, and Dave . . . otherwise known as the Moffatts. We just wanna say thanx for being the fiercest fans any band could ever have! And we've got to send out x-tra appreciation for buying our book — once you read it, you'll be completely clued in on everything from facts to faves! Have fun . . .

TABLE OF CONTENTS

CHAPTER 1

A NEW BEGINNING

Scott, Clint, Bob, and Dave: four super sibs from one talented family. How'd these bros break out to become tha bomb? Read on . . .

On March 30, 1983, little Scott Moffatt made his first appearance, in Whitehorse, Yukon, Canada. Less than a year later, on March 8, 1984, triplets Clint, Bob, and Dave showed up to keep him company. And . . . a band was born.

DAVE: "We're really happy with what we're doing right now. We don't exactly feel the need to live a 'normal' life. It's a lot of hard work, but sometimes it's really relaxing, too. It's pretty cool."

Well, not quite yet. But both of their parents are musicians, so there were always tunes playing in the Moffatt house. According to Dave, "We grew up listening to a lot of classics and some country music, too — the Beach Boys, Elvis Presley, Dwight Yoakam, Garth Brooks."

And it didn't take long for the 'rents to notice that there was something seriously special going on with their offspring. "Our first start as musicians was probably when my mom was rehearsing a song from the animated movie *An American Tail*," remembers Bob. "She was going to perform it at a local beauty pageant. Dave just took the mike and started singing. He was only three, but he knew all the words."

MOPPET MOFFATTS: "Big bro" Scott [top] was almost two; the triplets [l. to r] Clint, Bob, and Dave had just turned one.

Scott, Clint, Bob, and Dave — can you tell who the identical twins are?

Seeing how his kid kicked it out on the mike, Dad Frank Moffatt suggested Dave join Mom at the pageant. Not one to be left out of a good thing, four-year-old Scott piped up and demanded to go, too.

Dave wowed the crowd, but Scott's big break would have to come a little later. He was so hyper backstage, the show's manager was afraid to let him go on! Fortunately he got another chance; the boys did a telethon for a local children's charity, and then Scott appeared in a toy commercial. What did he do with his first paycheck? Bought a guitar, of course!

After that, the fierce foursome made all sorts of appearances at music fests and charity events for places like hospitals, schools, and senior citizens' homes. In 1992, they spent their summer crossing Western Canada, where they met Alan Osmond, a country music singer. Alan invited the boys to play

with his family, the Osmonds, at their show in Branson, Missouri. During this time, the guys also recorded their first album, *It's a Wonderful World*.

Soon they scored regular gigs in Las Vegas and Branson, and even snagged a slot on *Nashville Now*, on the TNN network. In December of 1994, they

SCOTT: "When we signed our record deal in 1994, our dad sat us down and made sure we understood that we'd made a commitment for a certain amount of time. But then he said that when the contract ended, we'd have to decide if we wanted to keep going. He said we could go back to school, play sports, and do our own thing. But we all wanted to pursue music, and I'm glad we did."

became the youngest band ever to sign a major label recording contract. Their second album, *The Moffatts*, was one of the top-selling country albums of 1995. Not bad for a bunch of eleven-year-olds!

By 1996, the guys were becoming a lot more interested in rock than in country. They moved to another

Tot Scott got his first guitar at the age of five.

label, called EMI. In October of 1997, they began recording their first rock/pop album. Maybe you've heard of it . . . it's called *Chapter I: A New Beginning*. Clint came up with that name because he wanted people to know that there *would* be more chapters in the Moffatts musical career — and that the Moffatts musical style had a new beginning by changing from country to rock/pop.

Like a lot of bands, the Moffatts road-tested their new sounds by touring Europe and Asia. Unlike most bands, they were super-successful wherever they went. They sold out shows in places like Switzerland, Germany, Spain, Thailand, the Philippines, and Malaysia, and had gold albums all across the world — which means that before their latest CD was even released here, they'd already sold over a million copies of it. Now that they're touring the U.S., they'll be adding one more country to their list of conquests!

MUST-KNOW MOFFATT INFO!

■ Because the Moffatts tour year-round, they're home-schooled. Their parents teach them in each subject, and then they send their homework back to a central office in Canada to be graded.

■ You may be able to tell them apart now, but Clint and Bob actually look exactly the same behind the different threads and 'dos. They're identical twins as well as being triplets with Dave.

■ For three weeks of every year, the Moffatts are all the same age — Scott was only born eleven months and one week before his baby brothers.

■ The Moffatts all play by ear; they've never had singing or music lessons!

■ When Scott was six and the triplets were five, they met a street performer who told them he made eighty dollars a day. The boys begged Dad to let them sing outside, and they made over eight hundred dollars the first day!

■ Dad used to dress all four alike, because he said if one kid got lost, it would be easier to find him. That's cool — but did he have to dress them in neon green shorts and pink T-shirts?

THAT WAS THEN: As country singers [in 1996] the bros [left to right] Scott, Bob, Clint, and Dave, posed in a Nashville trolley.

CLINT: "Education is really important to us. We're going to go to college no matter what, even if it's not right away."

THIS IS NOW: Rockers, Dave, Scott, Bob, and Clint do a promo appearance at LA's hip KISS-FM radio station.

the moffatts
SCOTT

CHAPTER 2

SCOPING OUT SCOTT

Born almost a year before triplets Clint, Bob, and Dave, big brother Scott can be the hardest to pin down. "I'm very fickle," he admits. "I like to keep moving around, I like change. I go from style to style." The poet of the posse, he's also the shiest. He'd rather sit back and watch than do all the talking, and he's happiest hanging out, writing songs, and drawing "whatever comes out of my mind, like abstract stuff." (He plans to open his own art gallery one day.) Since he's the creative kid, it's no shock that his job is to help oversee the songwriting and producing of the albums.

Put him alone in a room with his acoustic guitar and some Nirvana CD's, and he's thrilled to just chill. But . . . get him on stage, and he morphs into a wild man; when it comes to live shows, he has to 'fess up: "I bring a little bit of an attitude to the band. I can be the craziest up there. I don't know when to stop."

At an acoustic show, Scott sings "Until You Loved Me."

"I have this dream to own an island in the Caribbean, where I'd be the governor. I'd have one area just for clubs, another one for restaurants, and a third for shops. The whole thing would be surrounded by the beach. I'd call it Moffatt."

ATTACK of the Killer "M"

An example of a Scott Moffatt original drawing!

Back in his bedroom in 1996, Scott strummed away.

SCOTT'S STATS

Full Name: Scott Andrew Moffatt
Birthday: March 30, 1983
Birthplace: Whitehorse, Yukon, Canada
Family Status: Oldest brother
Eyes: Blue
Hair: Long brown with blond streaks

Clint on Scott:
"Scott's very spontaneous. He's just wild on stage. One time he went on with leather pants and a leather vest, no shirt underneath. These days he dresses a little classier."

FAVES

Moffatts' Song: "Misery." It's a little more aggressive than most of our tunes.
Song: "Smells Like Teen Spirit" (Nirvana)
Album: *OK Computer* (Radiohead)
Movie: *Twelve Monkeys*
Cartoon Character: Bugs Bunny
Cereal: Lucky Charms
Team: Dallas Cowboys
Month: December, because it's cold and I love to ski.

FAST FACTS

Most Prized Possession: My guitars
Musical Influences: Nirvana, Bush, Beatles, Elvis
Pet Peeve: When people interrupt me
Freaked Out By: Heights. Well, actually, falling from heights!
Worst Habit: Cracking my knuckles

"I may be older than the others, but I'm definitely not their guardian! We all look after each other. If they're going to get in trouble, I'll let them know and help them out, but it's not like I always have my eyes on them."

QUICK Q&A

Q: What one thing makes you happiest?
A: Creating music. You know what else would make me happy? Turning on the radio 20 years from now and hearing one of our songs on an oldies station!

Q: What do you really groove on, musically?
A: Playing live gigs. It's such a great vibe. By the end of the show you're at the point where you don't really have control. It's hard to stop yourself from, you know, going nuts on stage. We love it when the audience goes crazy, too. We want them to be jumping around having a good time just like we are.

Q: If you weren't a musician what would you be?
A: I think I'd be a soccer player. I love soccer. But I get so tired from it, if I do it once a month I'm happy. So maybe I'd be an artist instead!

SHY SCOTT

"If I don't know people, I have a hard time talking to them, so a lot of the time I come across as snobby or whatever. But it's just shyness. Sometimes I'd just rather hang back and observe than talk."

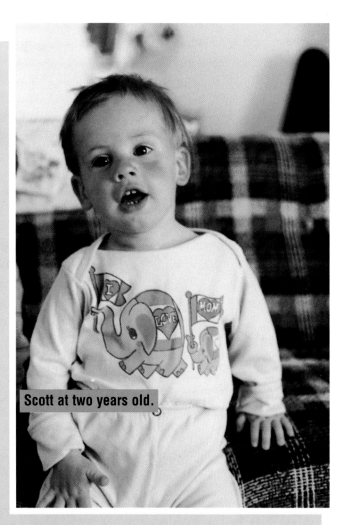

Scott at two years old.

Going up! The band, in an elevator, is heading for the top!

11

the moffatts
CLINT

CHAPTER 3

CLUE IN TO CLINT

Clint is extra-intense, and he'll do whatever it takes to get the other guys to see things his way. The most business-minded in the group, the band's bass player could also be the Moffatts' manager — if he didn't already have enough to do. He works on their concert arrangements, which means thinking of everything from security to catering (when he has his choice, they make it Mexican).

Clint's head is forever filled with statistics, whether it's the latest number of gold and platinum records they've had (fourteen, all overseas so far) or the scores for his top team (the Dallas Cowboys). The neatest and most organized member of the band, his clothes are always perfectly folded and ready for the next gig, interview, or photo shoot. So it's scarcely a shock that he's the member most likely to be spotted in a suit (his outfit of choice since he was ten, according to Bob).

Meeting hockey great Wayne Gretzky was major for the little Moffatts—left to right, Scott, Clint, Dave, and Bob.

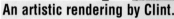

An artistic rendering by Clint.

CLINT'S STATS

Full Name: Clinton Thomas John Moffatt
Birthday: March 8, 1984 at 1:02 PM
Birthplace: Vancouver, British Columbia, Canada
Family Status: Oldest triplet, Bob's twin
Eyes: Brown
Hair: Short brown with blond on top

Scott on Clint:
"Clint's the neatest. If you open his suitcase, everything's perfectly in order. You can just close it right up again. I have to stand on mine and jump on it to get it shut."

FAVES

Moffatts' Song: "Written All Over My Heart," because it's newer. I'm a big fan of new things.
Song: "Heaven" (Bryan Adams)
Album: *Reckless* (Bryan Adams)
Movie: *Ace Ventura, Pet Detective*
Cartoon Characters: Beavis and Butthead
Cereal: Corn Pops
Team: Dallas Cowboys
Month: March, because it's my birthday month!

FAST FACTS

Most Prized Possession: My basses
Musical Influences: Bryan Adams, Beatles, Garth Brooks, Beach Boys
Pet Peeve: When someone refuses to drop an argument after it's over
Freaked Out By: I'm not a big worrier, but if I had to say, maybe airplanes.
Worst Habit: Cracking my knuckles

QUICK Q&A

Q: How did you decide to dye your hair?
A: Actually, Scott had the idea first. He wanted his own style, so he came home one day and asked our step-mom Sheila to bleach the front of his hair. As he was doing that, my dad asked if I wanted to shave my head. And I said sure, why not, it's something new. And I ended up dyeing the front of it while I was at it. I've been growing it out recently, though.

Q: What are your top tunes to cover?
A: It depends on the mood I'm in at a particular show. We cover "Shine," by Collective Soul, "Every Breath You Take," by the Police, "She Loves You," by the Beatles. My all-time favorite is probably "Sweet Home Alabama," by Lynyrd Skynyrd.

Bob on Clint:
"Clint's not as neat as he used to be, you know. When he was thirteen or fourteen, he used to wake up in the middle of the night and remake his bed."

"I'd love to be a quarterback for the NFL. I've always had a dream to kind of be like Troy Aikman, throwing the touchdown passes."

Q: What's the best part of touring for you?
A: I would say traveling. Before, I used to just sit in the bus and not even look out the window. But then our dad started grinding it into me that I was missing a lot. We have the opportunity to see millions of things that other people dream about. So now I try to really observe what's going on outside.

Q: How do you feel about being a role model?
A: It's something we definitely take into big consideration. We think about everything that we do. Sometimes we just do what normal brothers do and even if we're out in public we'll have a big argument. Which is the opposite of being a role model! It's hard sometimes, but it's cool, too. It's nice to be looked at that way.

KILLER Q&A

Bob, how'd you get that scar over your eye?
Bob: One time before a show Scott and I were play-fighting and I accidentally hit my head on a table. I had to go to the hospital and get five stitches. They got me back just in time to go on stage, and the host of the show announced it to everyone. And I was like, Well, this is kind of embarrassing. But it was kinda cool, too. I had a big Band-Aid over my eye. I looked like I was some mean warrior.

Do you still get goosebumps before a gig?
Clint: I get nervous before every single show. I used to say I didn't because I thought it was uncool. But honestly, yeah, I do. It's always the same time, too: five minutes before we go on. It's like hands squishing your stomach. And then when you get up on stage it's perfect. Because you're on the stage and it's your stage and there are people watching and you can do anything you want.
Scott: Frank Sinatra said that every time he walked on stage he'd get nervous. It's cool to get nervous because it adds to the excitement. It means that you still have that desire to go out on stage and, you know, love it.

What advice would you offer other aspiring musicians?
Dave: That it takes a long time to reach your goals! It also takes a lot of hard work, and once you start, you can't just give up a few days later. We've been singing for twelve years. Success definitely doesn't come overnight.

Why don't any of you have tattoos or pierces?
Scott: That's a decision made by all of us. We have a lot of fans in Southeast Asia, where tattoos and pierces aren't really approved of. Actually, I've always wanted a tattoo. I'd like to get a bracelet around my upper arm. But it won't happen in the next few years. If it does, I probably won't be thinking properly! I think my parents would be pretty angry at the beginning. They're not into that stuff. And there's a reason; I mean, why decorate yourself? There's no reason to. You should be happy with who you are.

Clint, at age one.

"I generally have to have my way. My favorite words have got to be 'I'm right.'"

the moffatts
BOB

CHAPTER 4

THE BREAKDOWN ON BOB

Seeing double? Nope. Clint and Bob are identical twins, and if Bob didn't leave his locks long, you might not be able to tell the two apart . . . at least until they opened their mouths! Clint may be super-extreme, but according to Scott, Bob's "so mellow it's unbelievable. He's like the typical California surfer dude" (except he's from Canada and hasn't yet learned to surf—though he plans on it). Maybe he takes his aggression out on his drum kit or the dance floor . . . Dave swears Bob boasts the Moffatts' maddest moves.

It's Bob's job to think about publishing and record sales, which must keep him pretty busy, since their four albums have sold nearly seven million copies. This laid-back lad is also the joker of the crew; he and Clint entertain the family with their own comedy act, and plan on starring in a big-screen comedy someday. "We're like the Dynamic Duo," Bob says. Once we get the humor going, there's no stopping us."

BOB'S STATS

Full Name: Robert Franklin Peter Moffatt
Birthday: March 8, 1984 at 1:04 PM
Birthplace: Vancouver, British Columbia, Canada
Family Status: Middle triplet, identical to Clint
Eyes: Brown
Hair: Long brown

Clint on Bob:
"Bob is the peacemaker of the group. We all have our moments, but Bob's the least likely to get carried away. That's why he's such a great part of the band. You know, we need that calming influence, instead of having all four guys ranting and raving!"

Little boy Bob displays his catch.

"I think everybody's born with a talent of some sort. They just have to find it and figure out how to use it." Bob includes original art as one of his talents.

FAVES

Moffatts' Song: "Written All Over My Heart"
Song: "So Much to Say" (Dave Matthews Band)
Album: *The Color and Shade of Things* (Foo Fighters)
Movie: *Good Will Hunting*
Cartoon Character: Beavis and Butthead
Cereal: Cocoa Puffs
Team: Dallas Cowboys
Month: December — 'Tis the season to be jolly!

FAST FACTS

Most Prized Possession: My necklace
Pet Peeve: Dave's snoring
Musical Influences: Beatles, Dave Grohl, Garth Brooks, Dwight Yoakam
Freaked Out By: A fear that the world will come to an end in the year 2000
Worst Habit: Cracking my knuckles

"You know how when you go out to eat you get a main course and a side order? Fame is like the side order. We want to be the best musicians possible, and that's always been our big goal. When we started, we didn't even think about fame or money. All we thought about was doing what we love and making good music. Sometimes fame comes with that, but it's never the most important part."

"I really don't have a specific style. It varies from day to day. But I wear a lot of stuff from a Canadian clothing company called Roots."

QUICK Q&A

Q: What's the craziest thing you've ever done?
A: We were doing a radio show in Nashville, and the DJs asked us if we'd go on a bungee jump at the Opryland theme park. We were like, we can't say no on the air! We were all freaking out, but we got on, pulled the rope, and went down. And it wasn't that bad. We went back three times in a row! Except Scott. He was chicken.

Bob has always been into hockey!

"I think if I hadn't become a musician I'd definitely have been a hockey player. Clint and I were really big hockey fanatics when we were younger. Whatever I did he wanted to do. But if you ask him he'll say it was the other way around!"

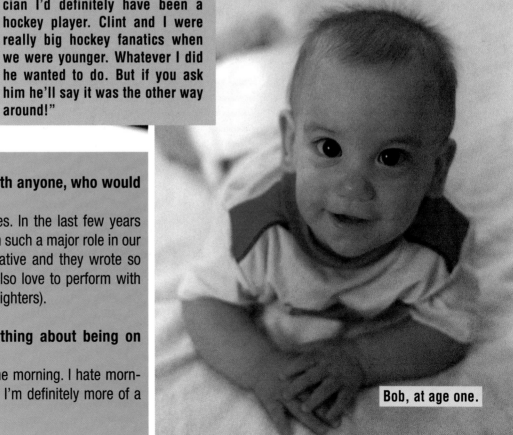

Bob, at age one.

Q: If you could jam with anyone, who would it be?
A: The remaining Beatles. In the last few years their music has taken on such a major role in our lives. They were so creative and they wrote so many great songs. I'd also love to perform with Dave Grohl (of the Foo Fighters).

Q: What's the worst thing about being on the road?
A: Waking up early in the morning. I hate mornings. I just can't get up. I'm definitely more of a night man.

the moffatts
DAVE

THE DEEP DISH ON DAVE

The baby of the bunch (by two minutes), keyboardist Dave's also the most hyper. He's easily the group's gabmeister, too. "He'll talk your ear off," Scott warns. Bob adds, "If you let him get going in a conversation, he's in heaven." The Moffatts' resident Romeo, he knows just what to say to anyone — especially girls. While his brothers kick the soccer ball around, Dave can usually be found flirting on the sidelines! Like Scott, Dave loves to draw; he'll doodle anywhere he can (including his school books).

Dave's the one who talks to their manager and record label about the band's videos and product endorsements (clothing companies take note: his dream endorsements are Versace and Bernini). Since he's a Batman fan, it's no surprise that he eventually wants to wind up on the big screen as an action hero.

Dave's the most outgoing Moffatt — his drawings are over the top, too.

DAVE'S STATS

Full Name: David Michael William Moffatt
Birthday: March 8, 1984 at 1:06 PM
Birthplace: Vancouver, British Columbia, Canada
Family Status: Youngest triplet
Eyes: Brown
Hair: Brown, short 'n' spiky

Bob on Dave:
"Clint's been wearing suits since he was ten, but Dave used to put on a T-shirt and sweats and think he was happening."

"Dave may be the group's Don Juan, but he has the worst luck. He's really good at knowing how to talk to girls, but whenever he asks them out something happens and they can't make it."

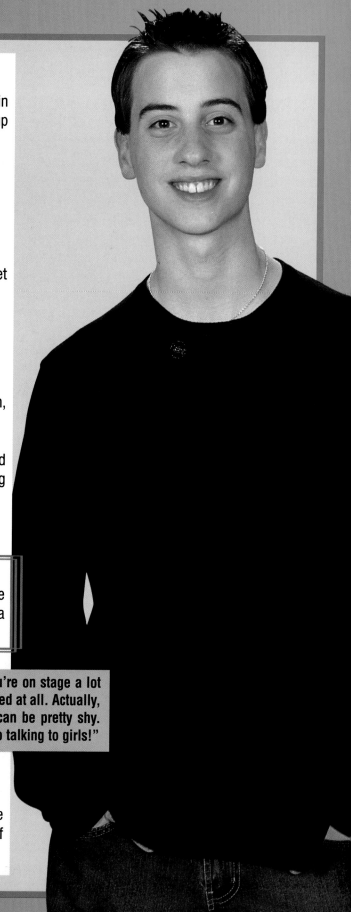

FAVES

Moffatts' Song: "Written All Over My Heart." It kicks in with a lot of energy, and it's a song the crowd jumps up and down on, which I think is really cool.
Song: "Nine Lives" (Aerosmith)
Album: *Get a Grip* (Aerosmith)
Movie: *Scream*
Cartoon Character: Batman
Cereal: Corn Pops
Team: Tennessee Titans
Month: December, because it's Christmas and we get to see our relatives

FAST FACTS

Most Prized Possession: My necklace
Musical Influences: Beatles, Bryan Adams, Aerosmith, Garth Brooks
Pet Peeve: Other people cracking their knuckles
Freaked Out By: Swimming in the ocean. I'm not afraid of the water — just all those unseen life-forms living in it!
Worst Habit: Snoring

Scott on Dave:
"Dave will chat up anybody, no matter who it is. If he saw the President he'd just go up to him and start a conversation."

"People think that if you're on stage a lot you don't get embarrassed at all. Actually, I'd say that offstage, I can be pretty shy. But not when it comes to talking to girls!"

QUICK Q&A

Q: What's your favorite subject in school?
A: English, because you have to read a lot and I like reading. I love scary novels, especially. I read a lot of Stephen King.

Q: What are the personality traits somebody needs to have to make it in the music industry?
A: Well, you have to be kind, and polite. You can't be rude. And you have to be real, too. If you're fake, no one takes you seriously.

Q: Have you had any mortifying moments on tour?
A: I've fallen off stage before! We were doing a gospel medley in Branson, Missouri. I was singing at the very edge of the stairs on stage. Well, that's where I was supposed to be. Instead my foot went right off the side. I heard a lot of laughter that night.

Dave, at age one.

In concert!

the moffatts

SCOTT, DAVE, CLINT, BOB

CHAPTER 6

THE MOFFATTS THEN AND NOW

Think the Moffatts are a new discovery? Then it's time for a reality-check rewind! Before they'd even made their latest album, the guys had played for the President at the White House, been on Nickelodeon and in tons of teen mags, and had a best-selling CD.

A LITTLE BIT COUNTRY . . .

Since their mom's a country music singer, the fab four grew up listening to a lot of that kind of music.

So natch, when they decided to follow in her footsteps, they did it as country singers themselves. From 1992 to 1996, they lived and recorded in Nashville, and spent several months in Las Vegas as part of a show called "Country Tonite."

During those years, the guys wore cowboy hats, fringed leather jackets with cow fur, and cowboy boots — a far cry from their threads today! They also did a lot of line dancing during their act, and even busted out special moves for their own dance, called the Caterpillar Crawl.

THEN: Okay — can you figure out who's who? Gotta be Scott, second from the left. Who's the baby in white? That'd be Dave, while twins Clint [left] and Bob [far right] complete the family picture.

In 1994, the band harmonized in the "Country Tonite" stage show in Branson.

. . . A LITTLE BIT ROCK AND ROLL

But as the guys grew, their tastes changed. "We weren't listening to country music anymore," Scott says. "Three or four years ago we started listening to bands like Nirvana and Metallica. Dave Matthews. And we wanted to play stuff that we were into. Which was rock music. We wanted to pick up instruments and, you know, play with distortion. Open it up wide, make it really loud."

Scott was a punk rocker in a 1989 TV commercial!

SCOTT: "When we played the White House I didn't think it was all that special. It was freezing, and boring for us. We were too young at the time to appreciate it; we wanted to be playing for kids our own age. But now I look back and I'm like, 'Man, that was a cool gig to do!'"

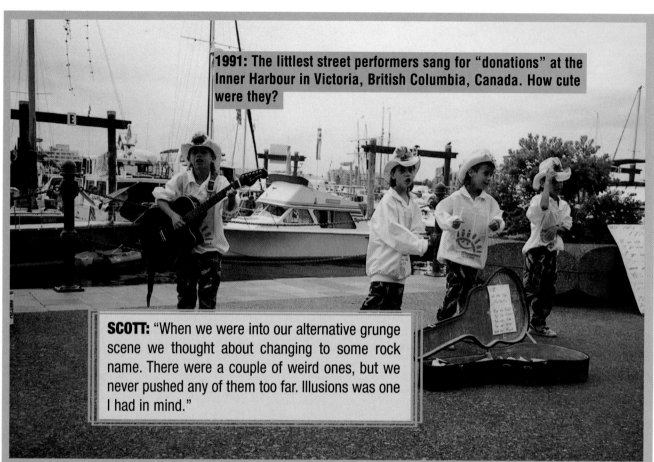

1991: The littlest street performers sang for "donations" at the Inner Harbour in Victoria, British Columbia, Canada. How cute were they?

SCOTT: "When we were into our alternative grunge scene we thought about changing to some rock name. There were a couple of weird ones, but we never pushed any of them too far. Illusions was one I had in mind."

1995: Fan Fair in Nashville: Bob, Scott, Dave, and Clint took a photo break.

DAVE: "Rock/pop is a lot more universal than country. When we went to Germany, people were like, 'What's country music?'"

Halloween, 1991: Scott was the little devil amid the "convicts," Bob (left), Clint, and Dave.

In 1989, the Moffatts wished their audience a very merry Christmas!

MOFFATT'S DATEBOOK: THE TIME OF THEIR LIVES

March 30, 1983: Sweet Scott plays his first live gig — in the delivery room!

March 8, 1984: First Clint's born at 1:02 pm . . . and then Bob at 1:04 pm . . . and finally Dave at 1:06 pm, the baby of the brood.

1985: At age 2, Scott starts slicking his hair back, pretending a spoon is a microphone. His father gives him the nickname "Elvis."

1986: Dave follows his big brother's lead, and begins singing into kitchen utensils for hours.

1988: As a Christmas present for their grandpas, the boys record their first song — at a karaoke studio in a mall! When they finish and look up, there are hundreds of people standing outside the studio watching them. Their first fans!

Performing at the Osmond Family Theater in 1992.

★Extra Info: The first song the Moffatts recorded was a cover of the Judds' "Grandpa."

1989: The cuddly cuties, now ages five and six, make their first-ever TV appearance, for the Timmy's Telethon in Canada. On Sunday afternoons, they sing at senior citizens' homes.

Scott does a commercial for Tomy Toys and uses the money to buy his first guitar.

1990: Bob snares his first drum kit, Dave commandeers his first keyboard, and Clint bags his first bass.

1991: The guys play over 100 performances, and start using their instruments onstage.

1992: Country singer Alan Osmond invites them to join his family's show in Branson, Missouri.

Singing for the United Way in 1990.

The 1995 Nashville Fan Fair.

Timmy's Springtime Telethon in 1993.

1998: Talk about a good year! They sell out concerts all over Europe and the Far East, and sell over a million records around the world.

The Moffatts television debut in 1989.

1993: They release *It's a Wonderful World*, and wrangle a weekly stint on a TV show called "Nashville Now." Then they head to the Aladdin Hotel in Las Vegas, to be part of a musical revue called "Country Tonite."

1999: The Moffatts record four new tracks for the U.S. version of *Chapter I: A New Beginning*. They release the album in America and . . . you know the rest!

1994: The Moffatts become the youngest band ever to sign a major label recording contract, with Polydor Nashville, and start making their second album, *The Moffatts*.

The Moffatts proudly sign with Polydor Nashville in 1994.

Playing the White Rock Music Festival in 1991.

A Moffatts fan club party in 1996.

1995: *The Moffatts* is one of the best-selling country albums of the year!

1996: The band releases its third album, *A Moffatts Christmas*, independently.

1997: They sign with a new label, EMI, and begin recording their first rock/pop album, *Chapter 1: A New Beginning*.

CHAPTER 7

NOT JUST ANOTHER BOY BAND

They're four musicians who happen to be teenagers — but whatever you do, please don't call Scott, Clint, Bob, and Dave a boy band. Here, in their own words, is why!

Why shouldn't we call you a "boy band"?

Scott: To us a boy band is a group of guys put together by management to look good. They don't play instruments or write music. A lot of the boy bands in Europe can't even sing! We do all those things, and more: we write songs, play instruments, coproduce our albums. We try to be as hands-on as possible. And we certainly weren't put together by some management team!

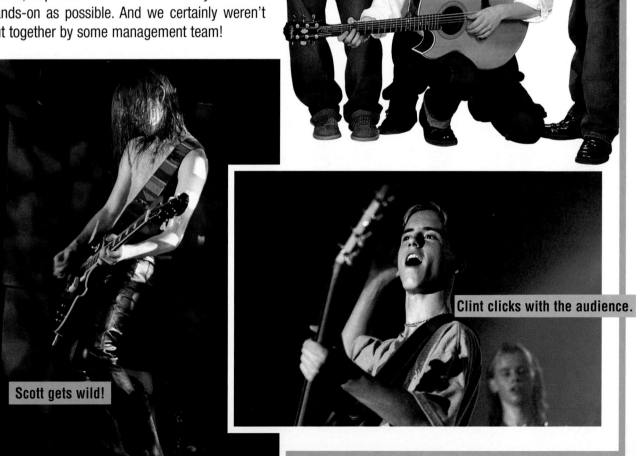

Scott gets wild!

Clint clicks with the audience.

Do a lot of people compare you to a certain other bunch of MMM-bopping brothers?

Scott: When we released *Chapter One*, plenty of people compared us to Hanson. But once we'd gone four times platinum, they stopped mentioning them in our interviews! There are some obvious similarities between us. Now, in Asia and the United Kingdom, journalists refer to us as the Beatles of the year 2000. Which we consider the greatest of compliments, but we feel we have a long way to go yet to be mentioned in the same breath as the Beatles.

Dave: Their music has more of a blues feeling to it. They have a lot of organ in their songs.

Bob: Whereas ours has more of an alternative rock edge. But they play their own instruments and write their own songs. And I think that's cool.

What are some more differences between you and other teen acts?

Scott: Our music isn't as slick and polished as a lot of the acts coming out now. We have guitars, real drums. Our harmonies are tight, but they aren't perfect. Which is good. A lot of acts try to be faultless in the studio, and then you go see them live and freak out, because they aren't even close to perfect. We try to leave some flaws in. It makes our music more real.

Do you hang with any other bands your age?

Bob: We know 'N Sync the best because we do a lot of shows with them in Europe. They're nice guys. Even though they've reached that massive multi-platinum level, they're totally down-to-earth. And they can really sing, too! You couldn't tag them a boy band, either. I'd call them a vocal group.

CHAPTER 8

OH, BROTHER!

The Moffatts may have morphed over the years, but there's one thing that never changes: they'll always be family, and they'll always be tight. "A lot of bands have problems they can't get over," observes Scott. "But you don't see many family bands go down because of things like drugs or alcohol. I think that's because you always have someone to talk to. You just can't talk to your friends the way you can talk to your brothers."

In fact, "all 4 one" could be the Moffatt motto. Stepmom Sheila handles the scheduling and home schooling, Dad's the show producer, and Mom Darlana flies out to be with them on different tour stops. Whenever there's a family decision to be

Bob on stage.

The karate kids kicked it — February 1996.

made, each person gets an equal vote. That goes for everything from which songs should go on an album to where they'll take their next vacation.

Of course, that doesn't mean it's all happy faces and rainbows on the Moffatts tour bus. "Oh, we fight like normal brothers — of course we do," Dave admits. "Like, if Bob takes my shirt and won't cop to it, there's an argument right there," he says with a grin. "When we fight, we fight about everything: what we're going to wear, which songs we want to work on, who's going to order what in a restaurant!" Scott laughs. "But five minutes later, things'll be perfectly fine."

One thing every member of this family always agrees on is the importance of helping others. From the first, Dad taught his boys that they would get more out of giving than receiving, and they believe it. Even though they're megastars around the world, they do several events a month for children's hospitals, schools, and other charities.

All four brothers wear identical gold necklaces given to them by a family friend. The necklace is in the shape of a circle, with the outline of a fish in the middle. According to Bob, the symbol represents "God first, other people second, and yourself third. That's how we try to think. Wearing it helps keep you down on the ground."

During a recent vacation in Hawaii, each family member got to vote on how to spend one day. Because Clint, Bob, and Scott all had the same idea, the whole family spent three days on the golf course! (Dave voted to go shopping!)

The triplets — Dave, Clint, and Bob — are king cutups.

QUICK Q&A

Q: Bob, are you and Clint totally tight since you're not only triplets, but twins?

Bob: Ever since we were young we've had a special bond, but we're not as fanatical as we used to be. We used to need everything to be exactly the same. If one of us had a Mars Bar, the other couldn't get a Snickers! We wore the same things, did the same things, lived in the same room. Our parents had to separate us because they were afraid we were too attached.

Q: Are there any advantages to being a triplet?

Clint: Not any more than just being four brothers. People see us together and they think it's kind of cool. But for us it just seems normal. The best thing is that we all have three friends around 24–7.

Q: Your parents decided that each of you should handle one area of your careers. Why?

Scott: So we could learn. They think of it as part of our education. I think it's smart to learn about the industry, so we can't get pushed around.

Dave: It's exciting to have your own job, too. We all have laptops and we e-mail the businesspeople we work with. I handle videos and endorsements, so when our manager finds a company that wants to work with us, he tells me and I talk to my brothers about the pros and cons.

Bob's totally into his new wheels.

Clint gets crowned.

CHAPTER 9

THE GIRL OF THEIR DREAMS

SCOTT

Want a Moffatt to miss you like crazy? Well, all four fly guys are flying solo these days, so listen up if you wanna hear 'em say'n I ♥ U.

Every Moffatt swears he's the romantic one. "People find romance in different places," Bob says. "Some people find it when they're really soft and warm. Other people find romance when they're being humorous and having fun." And what about him? "Actually, I think both ways are pretty romantic!" he admits.

Which Moffatt's the man for you? That depends on whether your idea of a perfect plan involves the beach or Beavis and Butthead!

THE GIRL OF MY DREAMS
Scott: I'd want to go out with someone who's confident, who dresses well, and takes care of herself. And can have a good time anywhere. You know, someone who can party one night and be into a mellow scene the next. I'd like to be with a person I can really talk to.

DREAM DATES
Scott: I think we'd just go for dinner at a little French place . . . in Paris! Then we'd walk around for a while, and find a cool café on a side street. We'd sit and have dessert — ice cream for me — and just talk, for hours. Maybe I'd write her a romantic song or poem, too.

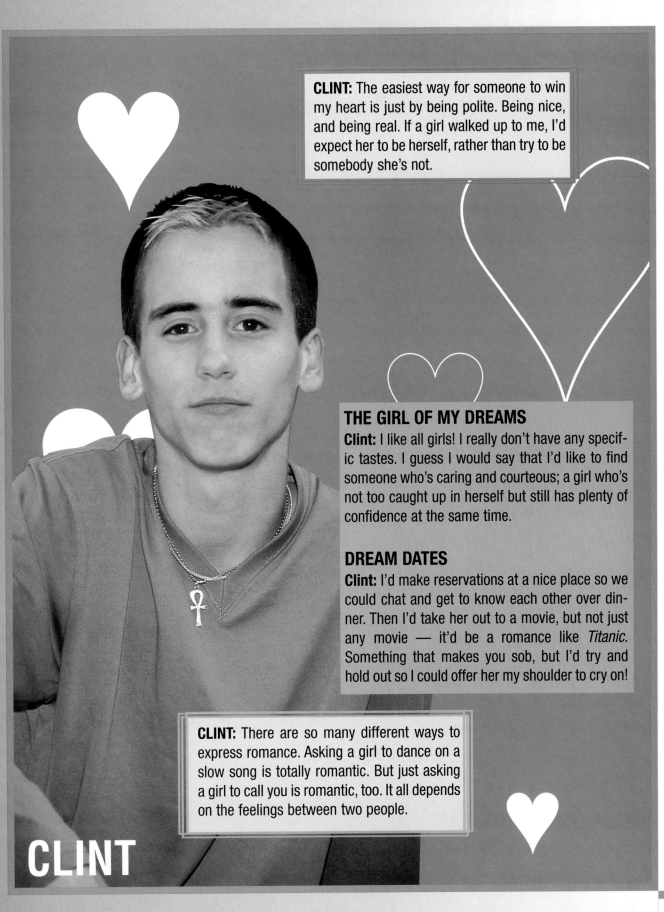

CLINT: The easiest way for someone to win my heart is just by being polite. Being nice, and being real. If a girl walked up to me, I'd expect her to be herself, rather than try to be somebody she's not.

THE GIRL OF MY DREAMS

Clint: I like all girls! I really don't have any specific tastes. I guess I would say that I'd like to find someone who's caring and courteous; a girl who's not too caught up in herself but still has plenty of confidence at the same time.

DREAM DATES

Clint: I'd make reservations at a nice place so we could chat and get to know each other over dinner. Then I'd take her out to a movie, but not just any movie — it'd be a romance like *Titanic*. Something that makes you sob, but I'd try and hold out so I could offer her my shoulder to cry on!

CLINT: There are so many different ways to express romance. Asking a girl to dance on a slow song is totally romantic. But just asking a girl to call you is romantic, too. It all depends on the feelings between two people.

CLINT

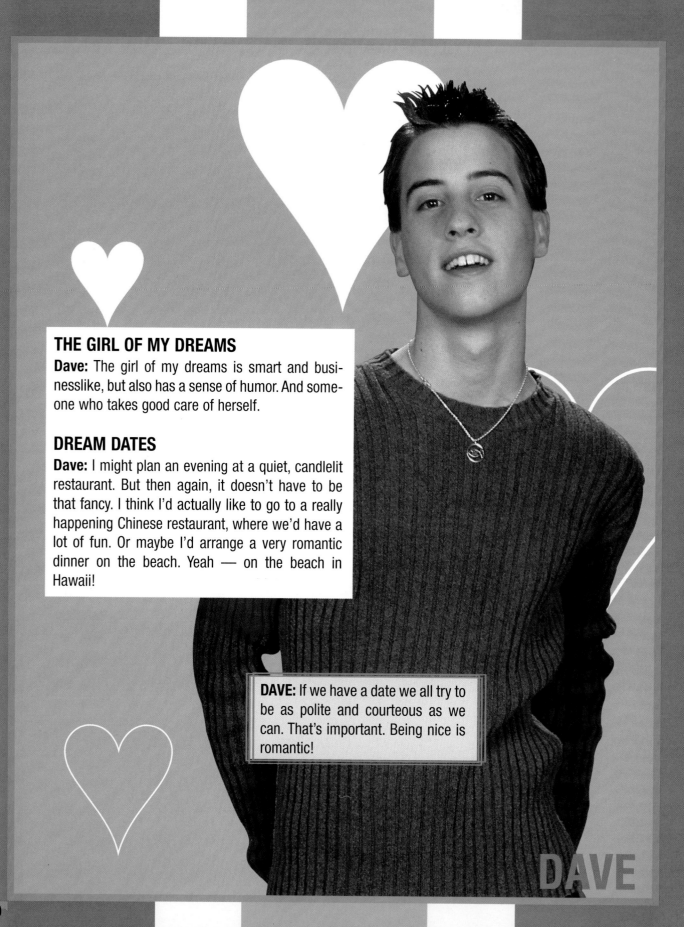

THE GIRL OF MY DREAMS

Dave: The girl of my dreams is smart and businesslike, but also has a sense of humor. And someone who takes good care of herself.

DREAM DATES

Dave: I might plan an evening at a quiet, candlelit restaurant. But then again, it doesn't have to be that fancy. I think I'd actually like to go to a really happening Chinese restaurant, where we'd have a lot of fun. Or maybe I'd arrange a very romantic dinner on the beach. Yeah — on the beach in Hawaii!

DAVE: If we have a date we all try to be as polite and courteous as we can. That's important. Being nice is romantic!

DAVE

THE GIRL OF MY DREAMS

Bob: The kind of girl I'd want to go out with? One who likes a drummer! No, I'd say a girl who's pretty casual, who likes to talk and have fun. And watch football. Oh, and she'd have to like Beavis and Butthead, too!

DREAM DATES

Bob: Well, first of all, I'd drive up in my Rolls (which I don't actually own yet). I'd come knockin' at the door with a dozen roses. Then we'd go out for a romantic, candlelit dinner, followed by a movie. A thriller, naturally, so my date can jump on my lap if she gets scared!

BOB: You know what's romantic? When you feel comfortable enough to just be yourself.

BOB

KICKIN' MOFFATTS QUIZ

So you think you're Moffatts mad? Take this kickin' Moffatts quiz to find out just how high you rate on the Moffatt-o-Meter. All the answers are somewhere in the book, but if you're really devoted you won't need to look!

1) It's Dave's turn to bond with the remote, and he's in the mood for some 'toons. This means the guys'll be spending the afternoon with:

a) Batman
b) X-Men
c) The Powerpuff Girls

2) You've just whipped up a batch of fresh fajitas. The doorbell rings. Which Moffatt is standing outside holding a bag of tasty tortilla chips and some slammin' salsa?

a) Clint
b) Dave
c) They all hate Mexican food. I'm making spaghetti and waiting for one of them to show up with garlic bread.

3) Dave may be the baby, but he's not the one with the baby blue eyes. Who is?

a) Bob
b) Scott
c) I thought they were all identical?!

How well do you know us? You're about to find out!

6) Since you did such a good job cleaning your room, Mom scored you a couple of seats to their upcoming sold-out show. What tune are you most likely to hear the cuties cover?

a) "2,000 Light Years from Home" (the Rolling Stones)
b) "Sweet Home Alabama" (Lynyrd Skynyrd)
c) "Home, Home on the Range" (some cowboy guy)

7) The Moffatts have been intensely influenced by the masterful musical stylings of:

a) Brian Setzer
b) Bryan Adams
c) Adam Sandler

4) The necklace each brother wears is in the shape of:

a) A fishing pole
b) An outline of a fish
c) Trey Anastasio, the guitarist of Phish

5) Your 'rents are right, you know: your room is a disaster area. Which mega-organized member of the Moffatts would you try to bribe into coming over for a cleanup session?

a) Clint
b) Scott
c) Frank

Scott

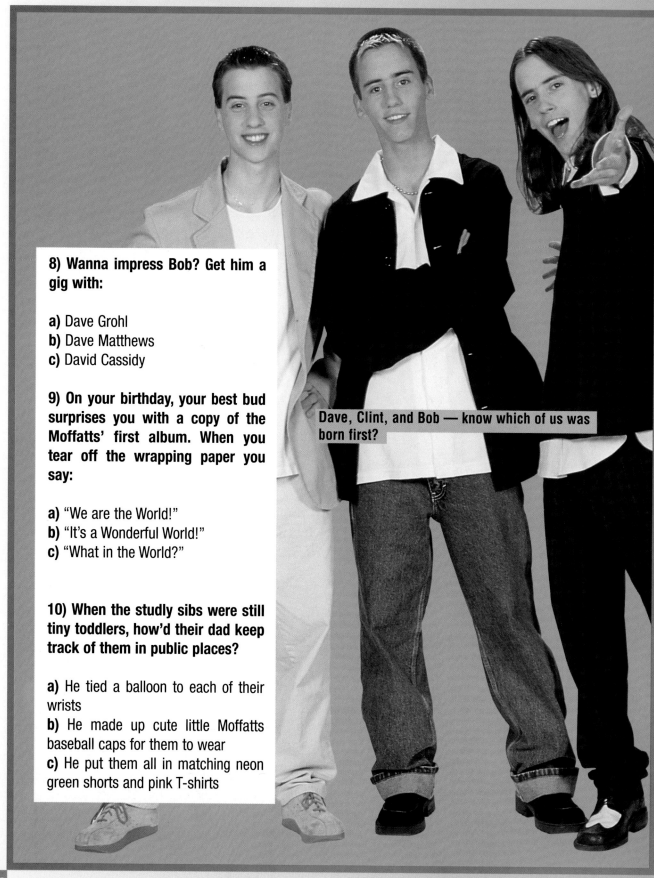

8) Wanna impress Bob? Get him a gig with:

a) Dave Grohl
b) Dave Matthews
c) David Cassidy

9) On your birthday, your best bud surprises you with a copy of the Moffatts' first album. When you tear off the wrapping paper you say:

a) "We are the World!"
b) "It's a Wonderful World!"
c) "What in the World?"

10) When the studly sibs were still tiny toddlers, how'd their dad keep track of them in public places?

a) He tied a balloon to each of their wrists
b) He made up cute little Moffatts baseball caps for them to wear
c) He put them all in matching neon green shorts and pink T-shirts

Dave, Clint, and Bob — know which of us was born first?

HOW'D YOU RATE?

1) a
2) a
3) b
4) b
5) a
6) b
7) b
8) a or b
9) b
10) c (We swear!)

MOFFATT-O-METER
Your score lands you:

In the upper balcony
1-3
Hmmm. Were you doing homework when you were supposed to be reading this book?

On the floor, near the aisle
4-7
Nice job! You're crazy for the Moffatts, all right; there's no doubt you'll be there for them when they come to town!

Front row, center
8-10
Congratulations! It's written all over your heart: You're a true-blue, mega-Moffatts-maniac!!!

Our bedroom, back in Nashville: we don't live there anymore.

Bob was in trophy city!

WITH LOVE, FROM US TO YOU!

SOME RANDOM, BUT MEANINGFUL THOUGHTS, STRAIGHT FROM THE HEART . . .

As long as identical twins Clint and Bob have totally different hair, it's easy to tell 'em apart.

"Every day presents a new challenge for us. We have a number one hit in one country and in another country they won't even play our song on the radio. We've learned to accept other people's opinions of us and realize not everyone has the same view on each subject. However for us we know that it's persistence and a commitment to excellence that builds long-term success and not a lucky break."
— Clint Moffatt

"Our dad told us a long time ago that we should never compete with anyone in the music business, but we had better be as good musically as everyone who has made it in the music business."
— Dave Moffatt

"It seems like every week something we're really looking forward to falls apart in the music business, which has taught us to focus on the big picture, never give up, and keep things in perspective."
— Bob Moffatt

"When we were touring Southeast Asia we couldn't believe the living conditions of the poor, but what amazed us most, was that the poor children playing in the streets seemed to be so happy and full of life."
— Dave Moffatt

"When I was about six years old I had a dream that we were performing in front of a crowd so large that I couldn't see the end of it. Our dad felt that he should consider our interest in music more seriously after that."
— Scott Moffatt

"We were scheduled to sing the national anthem at a Los Angeles Kings game in 1990, but when we got there they said that they had scheduled someone else to sing. We really wanted to sing and watch Wayne Gretzky play. We cried all the way back to the hotel."
— Bob Moffatt

"We've been compared to the Osmonds, the Jackson 5, the Beatles, Hanson, and the Bee Gee's. The best part is they've all had huge success."
— Scott Moffatt

"The Moffatts are no different from everyone else. Everyone has a special talent, it's just that some people aren't paying attention to theirs."
— Clint Moffatt

"When I first came up with the idea for 'Frustration,' I envisioned a sane person trapped inside of an insane asylum with no way out. My dad really liked the idea but wanted to write it from the perspective of a teenager, who is trapped within the frustration of not being heard or understood. The final outcome is one song with two different stories."
— Scott Moffatt

"'Raining in My Mind' was the first song we co-wrote with Glen Ballard. To be honest we were a little intimidated, because after all he is one of the greatest songwriters and producers in the world and we had no idea how he felt about working with four teenagers. But within minutes we were totally comfortable in the studio. To this day, the first session with Glen is one of my fondest memories in music and what's even better, I really, really, like playing the song live."
— Bob Moffatt

"I wrote 'Misery' while lying in bed, thinking about a girl that I had had a date with, and knew that because we traveled so much, would probably never be able to date again."
— Scott Moffatt

"The idea behind 'Over the Rainbow' is that there is always something more behind what you see and that what's obvious isn't always what it's made out to be."
— Clint Moffatt

"'Say'n I ♥ U' was the first song that the four of us wrote totally by ourselves. It was originally arranged more like a Nirvana or Bush song, but Scott got this idea a week or so before we went into the studio to switch the arrangement to ska. We wrote the song at our management's office in about an hour and a half."

"This shot is from our album art — it's one of our favorites. Hope you like it, too."

A MESSAGE FROM THE MOFFATTS

So now you know the score on all four of us! Hope you had a blast reading our story — we've sure had fun living it!

What's up next? Well, we've been tweaking some new tunes, and we plan to start recording a rad new album early next year. It'll still be rock/pop, but expect some surprises — we're always changing and exploring, and we try to make sure our music does, too. Until then, we'll be traveling all across the country . . . and hoping to hear from you along the way!

Oh, and by the way, thanx for calling the radio stations and The Box to request our songs and videos!